Rocky Mountain Summer

by Linda Baxter

Cover Illustration: Doug Knutson
Inside Illustration: Larassa Kabel

About the Author

Linda was born in Cheyenne, Wyoming, and traveled with her military family, finally settling in Tempe, Arizona. She graduated with a degree in elementary education from Arizona State University. Linda taught elementary grades in Phoenix, Arizona, and Catshill, Bromsgrove, England.

She lives with her husband, Dave, and three children in Monte Sereno, California.

Text © 1998 by Perfection Learning® Corporation.
Printed in the United States of America.
For information, contact
Perfection Learning® Corporation,
1000 North Second Avenue,
P.O. Box 500,
Logan, Iowa 51546-0500.
PB ISBN-10: 0-7891-2162-x ISBN-13: 978-0-7891-2162-2
RLB ISBN-10: 0-7807-6790-x ISBN-13: 978-0-7807-6790-4

6 7 8 9 10 PP 12 11 10 09 08

Contents

1
Goodbye, Ma

Gran and Paw stood together on the wooden sidewalk. The wagon towered above them. They waited as Fern sobbed into her mother's arms. Roy turned away so that no one would see his trembling lip.

Ma held Fern's tear-streaked face in her hands. She looked into Fern's eyes. "Fern, I know this is hard for you. It's hard for me too. But we don't have a choice right now. I've got to work. And this isn't a place for children to live. You know that Gran and Paw will take good care of you and Roy." Fern's mother held her close in a hug and whispered, "Remember, sometimes you can't choose how things are. But you *can* choose how you look at them."

Ma hugged Fern one last time. Fern climbed into the front of the wagon. Ma hugged Roy so hard that neither of them could breathe for a moment. Gran and Paw had already climbed aboard with Fern. Roy climbed into the back of the wagon.

There was hardly any room for Roy to sit. The supplies were stacked high on all sides of the canvas-covered wagon. They had to take everything they would need for the entire summer.

Roy's eyes finally adjusted to the dim light. He could see Aunt Hattie sitting on a chest, quietly watching him. Aunt Hattie smiled at Roy. With a heavy heart, Roy turned to watch out the back as the wagon lurched forward.

Roy peered up at the huge building where Ma would be working. It was the famous Brown Palace Hotel. It was the tallest and fanciest thing Roy had ever seen. Ma had shown them around inside. She was going to be a cook in the hotel restaurant. It was a good job, and they needed the money.

Roy and Fern had never been apart from their mother. Roy was eleven now, and Fern would be ten in September. They had all lived with Gran and Paw for many years. Now the two children must go with their grandparents into the Rocky Mountains for the summer.

Roy looked through an opening to the front of the wagon. He watched Gran and felt comforted. Gran was a round woman, always bustling about. Her brown hair, heavily streaked with gray, was pulled into a bun. She wore a plain gray work dress and a wide-brimmed bonnet. But even with this protection, her face was browned from a lifetime of outdoor work. Her hands were skilled and powerful. Kind gray eyes and a ready smile softened Gran's face, which was lined with care and hard work.

Paw was a mystery to Roy. Paw never talked much. Roy never knew what Paw was thinking. Sometimes, Roy didn't even want to know. It wasn't that Paw scared Roy, he just puzzled him.

Paw was still a powerful man. His eyes were bright blue under bushy white brows. His beard was streaked with white. His hair was long and gray.

Aunt Hattie was just Aunt Hattie. She couldn't talk, but she understood what everyone said. Her thin, quiet face told little of what she thought or felt. Her large gray eyes hid behind round, wire-rimmed glasses. Her mouse-colored hair was pulled tightly at the nape of her neck.

7

Although Ray and Fern had met Aunt Hattie before, they hadn't quite learned to be comfortable with her.

Fern had stopped crying now. She crawled back to sit with Roy on the bags of feed. Together they watched the city disappear behind them. Some people said Fern was skinny. Roy thought her small heart-shaped face was pretty. She and Roy both had blue eyes and light hair like Ma's. Roy's hair was always going the wrong way, while Fern's was caught in two long braids.

"I miss Mama already," Fern said.

Roy's heart ached, but he put on a brave face for his little sister. "It'll be fine, Fern. This'll be a great adventure. We've never been in the Rockies before. Maybe we can learn to hunt or fish in a stream. Maybe we'll find a hideout." Fern's face brightened a bit.

"And it's only for a little while, Fern," Roy continued. "Paw said that we would be back before two months."

"That seems like two forevers," said Fern with a heavy sigh.

They rode on in silence. The wagon, pulled by four huge horses, moved away from the noise of the city. It crept into the farmland between Denver and the Rockies. Sometimes a rider on horseback passed them. They even passed a few wagons that were on their way to the city.

They were headed into the mountains to chop saplings for fence posts. The wagon would be their home for the summer. Roy had decided to make it an adventure. He wanted to make Fern feel better about leaving Ma. Roy wanted to feel better about it too.

They traveled north and west all day. Before them, the mountains rose up to blend with the sky. Fern had to bend her neck back to see their snow-covered tops.

"Paw, how will we get up there?" she asked.

"There's a pass just after the river. It'll take us about two days to get up to the first camp. Tomorrow we'll cross the river. Then we'll make our way to the head of the pass."

It was getting late as they neared a stand of trees beside a small stream. "This will make a good stopping point," said Paw.

They all climbed down from the wagon. After the bumpy wagon ride, it felt good to be on solid ground again.

Paw helped Gran down from the wooden front seat. Then he said to Roy, "Go hunt us up some wood for the night. Fern, you help Gran and Hattie unload the supplies."

Soon everyone was busy. This would be their home for the night.

The sun finally hid behind the mountains. There would still be a few hours of twilight, but the air was cooling quickly. Roy soon had the cooking fire started. A sharp crack from beyond the wood meant there would be fresh meat for dinner. Paw was a good shot. They might have a rabbit or a prairie hen.

After supper, Roy helped Fern clean up their few metal dishes. "Roy, what did Ma mean today about choices?" Fern asked.

Roy thought about her question and answered slowly. "I'm not sure. But I think it has something to do with how you look at things. Sometimes there's no easy way to do a thing. Like when Ma decided to leave Dad. She decided we needed to come live with Gran and Paw instead of staying in Kansas." Roy shrugged his shoulders, unsure of how to explain it.

Both children were lost in their own thoughts as they finished the dishes.

The children would be sleeping in the wagon for the summer. But it was too crowded with supplies tonight. So they slept by the campfire. It was a clear night. As the fire died to a red glow, they could see the Milky Way spread across the sky.

"Do you ever see pictures in the stars?" asked Fern. But Roy was already asleep. Fern snuggled under the rough, warm blanket.

2
Adventures Begin

Paw was up early the next morning. He called to the children, "C'mon now. We have a river to cross."

Fern and Roy helped Paw get the horses ready to travel. Then after chores and a quick breakfast of cold corn bread, they climbed into the wagon.

It was mid-morning before they reached the river. Since it was late spring, the river was still high. The melting snow on the mountains above rushed along the banks, churning mud. This was where the river was the most shallow. But it was very wide.

On some rivers, wagons were carried across on large rafts. But the Platte River was shallow. So a wagon could make it across without rafts. A team of men would help them make the crossing.

Paw got down from the wagon. "Make sure that everything is inside and lashed down," he called back. "Gran, you drive the team. I'll lead them with that fellow's horse."

From the far side of the river, a person on horseback splashed into the water. He was carrying a coiled rope and leading another horse. Both horses waded into the stream and were soon belly-high in the icy cold water. With shouts from the rider, the horses eventually climbed the near bank. As the rider came closer, Fern and Roy could see that it was a woman.

She handed the rope to Paw and said, "Morning. My name's Polly. Lash this to the front of the wagon. We have a pulley on the far side that'll help get you across. Hurry, though. The river's been rising this morning. It's been warm enough on the mountaintops to melt snow."

The horses bravely splashed down the mud bank. Paw was riding an old workhorse that crossed the river many times a day. With loud shouts and a few cracks of the whip, Paw's team was soon belly-deep. It was difficult for them to stand in the current, much less pull the wagon. The noise from the rushing water drowned out all voices.

Polly put another rope around the lead horse and began pulling him across. Although they were drifting downstream, they were making progress. A team of mules on the far side was helping to drag the wagon closer.

Fern was hanging on to Gran's arm. She watched in horror as the muddy water washed around her ankles in the wagon. Fern was sure they would never make it. She pulled up her feet and clung tightly to Gran. Aunt Hattie, sitting in the back, was trying to keep the water from reaching their supplies. The wagon drifted sideways.

Finally, they were across. The horses found their footing on the banks and hauled everyone to safety. Fern smiled at Polly.

Polly looked very relieved. "I don't think any more wagons will be crossing for a while. That was too deep."

Fern and Roy were glad to be shaking the water out of their shoes.

After giving the horses a rest, they were ready to continue. Fern and Roy walked beside the wagon. The horses were pulling slowly now. The road was steeper.

Wildflowers were everywhere. Blue columbine and lupine, bright orange poppies, and yellow buttercups grew along the road. Fern wanted to gather enough for a bouquet. But she soon realized that when she picked a wildflower, it wilted and lost its beauty. She would just have to enjoy them growing along the road.

Fern noticed the forests of deep green pine and bright aspen. She and Roy walked beside the wagon as it crossed small creeks, rushing with snow melt.

Later as they hiked along, Fern asked Roy, "Why do the mountains look blue when you look at them from far away? And then they are covered with green when you see them up close?"

Roy rolled his eyes. It seemed to him that Fern always had too many questions. They were hard to answer too.

As afternoon faded to long twilight, the travelers came upon a large meadow. "This is Daniel's Meadow," said Paw. "We'll camp here tonight."

They pulled the wagon to the far side of the meadow. They stopped on a small rise. The children jumped out of the wagon and began their chores. It felt good to get out and do something.

Everyone was tired. And as darkness settled its soft summer quilt over them, they found sleep.

———————————

At the first streaks of dawn, Roy awoke to the sound of muffled sobs. He reached over to comfort his sister. He looked out over the dewy meadow. "Fern, look!" he whispered. "Look at all the elk."

In the meadow, a herd of elk was grazing on the spring grass. There were bulls with proud antlers and cows with new calves. A large bull stood away from the rest. His head was raised and his eyes were watchful while the others grazed. Roy grabbed Fern's arm.

"Look over by that brush. See? It's a mountain lion," he whispered.

The cat was stalking the elk herd. It headed for a cow and calf grazing near the edge of the herd. Fern held her breath as the lion moved in closer.

Then Fern jumped up and began to shout. She waved the blanket she had slept in, shouting, "Go, go, go!"

Roy joined in. He began to whoop and wave his hands over his head. The herd of elk quickly scattered. They were gone from the meadow in an instant. The lion darted back into the woods. She would have to find her breakfast somewhere else.

"What's going on here?" asked Gran from the tent. "Are you children all right?"

"We scared off a cougar!" shouted Roy. "You should have seen her run. She was going to eat one of the elk."

"She was sneaking up on the mother and her baby. But we spooked them," chimed in Fern.

Paw was awake by this time and said, "That lion has to feed her young too."

"But Paw," cried Fern, "she was going to get the baby!"

Paw shook his head and said, "It's always best when man leaves nature alone."

"My goodness! You gave me such a start, children," said Gran. "Go and gather some more wood, will you? We need a hot breakfast before we start today."

Roy and Fern put on their shoes and started off as Gran said, "Don't go out of sight. That cougar is still hungry."

As the children loaded their arms with wood, Roy asked Fern, "Were you crying again?"

Fern sighed, "Yes. I miss Mama. I want to go home."

Roy said, "You know we can't go back now. Let's just try to have some fun. C'mon, maybe Aunt Hattie will make pancakes."

And that's just what she did. Fern had to admit that pancakes tasted even better when you ate them by a fire in a beautiful meadow. She ate five and Roy ate seven.

"These are great, Aunt Hattie," said Roy as he wolfed down another.

He saw Aunt Hattie smile and then look away. They decided to leave the last one for the cougar. Paw only shook his head. But as Paw turned away, Roy saw him smile.

3
First Camp

Roy and Fern rode on the back end of the wagon. They watched the meadow disappear behind the trees.

The road ahead cut through rolling foothills and crossed many brooks. Sometimes the rock walls along the road were gray or black. At other times, they were a deep red color with dark stripes running through them.

"Those rocks make me hungry. They look like bacon," said Roy.

"I think you're always hungry," said Gran with a chuckle.

Ahead, like a wall rising before them, were the Rockies. As they turned a sharp corner in the road, they could see the pass. High up on the far mountain, Fern could see the cut of the road.

"We have to go up there?" squeaked Fern.

"Oh, boy!" cried Roy.

"You children will have to walk now," said Paw. "The horses already have enough of a load for the climb."

Gran was climbing down from the wagon. "I'll walk with you," she said. "Let's see if we can see some animals. Maybe we can learn about some of the plants too."

She handed a canteen to each of the children. "Here. I filled this at the stream this morning. It's icy cold. You should drink the whole canteen as we walk along. Look over there in the pine, Fern. Do you see the blue jay? Do you hear his call? He is warning us to stay clear of his mate."

The children walked alongside Gran. Aunt Hattie walked a bit ahead. It seemed a fine adventure. Fern was so happy she began to skip.

"Fern," said Gran with a smile, "I'm glad to see your smile, but go slowly and save your energy. We have a long walk ahead. Come and help your old Gran along."

Fern took Gran's warm strong hand and settled to a slow, even pace. Paw walked beside the horses. He drove them forward with their heavy load.

The roadside began to drop away as they climbed higher. They could look out over the green landscape. The air was so clear that they could see for miles.

"Can we see Denver?" said Roy as they rounded a curve and looked east.

"The foothills are in the way some, but look through those two trees," said Paw. "That's Denver."

"Hello, Mama!" called Fern. A faint echo came back to her.

"Let's do it together," said Gran.

They all called together, "Hello, Mama!"

"I'll bet she heard that, Fern," said Paw.

Somehow it made Fern feel a little closer to her mother.

They had walked for a few hours now. Fern was very tired and held on to Gran's arm. It seemed she couldn't breathe very well. Gran was puffing a bit too. Paw's face was damp with sweat.

"Let's stop for a bit, Paw," said Gran. "The children are very tired."

The family set large rocks under the wheels of the wagon. They watered the horses which drank thirstily from the bucket. Then Fern and Roy gave the horses their feed bags.

They found a bit of shade next to the cliff wall and sat down. The five hungry travelers quickly finished the bread, cheese, and apples.

"Why is it hard to breathe?" asked Roy.

"We're high up on the mountain. The air is thinner here. So your body has to work harder to get enough air," explained Paw. "You must walk slowly and breathe deeply until you get used to it."

"I've never seen the sky that color of blue before," said Fern, looking up.

Then they heard some rustling behind them on the cliff, followed by a strange cry.

"What was that?" asked Roy.

The cry came again. As they looked up into the brown rock, they could see small furry animals peeking out.

"Oh, marmots! I love them. Remember, Paw? We saw them last year and didn't know what they were called," said Gran.

Paw looked up at the bright-eyed creatures and smiled. "Strange critters," he said.

"They sort of look like woodchucks," said Roy. "They make such a funny cry."

"They live up here above the timberline in large colonies," said Paw. "I don't think anybody bothers them much."

After a while, Paw said, "Time to move on."

Fern knew that Paw was tired by the stiff way he walked. Her feet hurt too. They slowly continued the march over the mountain pass. Fern was too tired now to even look at the wildflowers. The marmots chattered at them from above.

Paw looked over at Roy and Fern. "We're coming up on the narrowest part of the trail," Paw said. "I need you children to go on ahead. Go about a half mile to the big bent tree. Make sure that no other wagon is coming down the road. It's too narrow up ahead for two wagons to pass. Then you stay there, Roy. Fern, you come back and let us know when we can move ahead. Do you understand?"

"Yes, Paw," the children answered together.

They made the hike together. In some places, the road became so narrow that Fern wondered how they would fit the wagon. They were very high now and could look down on the mountains around them. They seemed layered one on top of the other in darkening shades of blues and gray. They looked almost flat, like a picture.

Above them the marmots squealed again.

"Oh, hush," said Fern as Roy smiled. Fern smiled back.

Soon they came to the bent tree. It looked as if it was always fighting against the wind. Roy thought it was losing the battle.

They hadn't met another wagon on the way up. Fern and Roy stopped to catch their breath at the bent tree. It took a few minutes.

Then Roy said, "Go on back now, Fern. It won't be a hard walk downhill."

Fern turned to go, giving her brother a smile and a wave. Roy reached out and gave her a quick hug.

"Careful now," warned Roy.

Fern began the walk back. As she rounded a corner and looked out over the mountains, she felt very much alone. It was so quiet that all she could hear were her own footsteps. At first, a chill came over her. But then she took a deep breath and gathered strength from the mountains around her.

She walked on to the wagon, smiling. She wanted to run with joy down the road. But she was afraid that she wouldn't be able to stop once she started.

"There is no one coming, Paw," shouted Fern as she neared the wagon.

Paw, Gran, and Aunt Hattie were resting in the shade of the wagon as Fern walked toward them.

"Good job, Fern," said Gran. "Come walk with me."

After another breathless walk, they reached the top of the pass. The horses, blowing and drenched in sweat, needed several gallons of water each.

"Look up there, Fern," said Roy when they reached the bent tree. "I've been watching that fellow for the last hour."

Roy pointed to a huge eagle that was circling above them.

"Isn't he beautiful!" cried Gran. "He must be a golden. Look how he rides on the rising air from the mountains."

"I think I'd like to go for a ride with him," said Fern.

For the first time in many hours, they could ride in the wagon again. Fern and Roy watched the eagle glide and turn as they sat in the back of the wagon. They followed the road as it went down into a forest of aspen and pine.

It was almost dark as Paw finally called to the horses to stop.

"This is First Camp," said Gran. "This'll be our home for a while."

They had stopped in a large clearing near a small stream. It was almost flat. But Fern could see that the forest climbed the hill above them. Fern and Roy helped their grandparents unload the wagon.

Then Roy went to find wood to build a fire. Fern arranged some large rocks and a plank to serve as a table. Paw and Roy put some of the larger logs in a circle near the fire. It soon seemed like a real home as Gran cooked a thick stew. They hadn't realized how hungry they all were.

There was one last loaf of bread that Gran had saved. "From now on, it will be biscuits or corn bread," she said.

"We don't mind your biscuits every night of the year," said Paw as he returned from tending the horses.

After a warm and filling dinner by the fire, it was time to sleep. Paw had pitched a tent for him and Gran and another for Aunt Hattie. Roy and Fern would sleep in the wagon. Even with blankets, the floor of the wagon was hard.

"Tomorrow, we'll make you some soft beds," said Gran.

Fern didn't even feel the hard wood. She was already asleep.

"Good night, Gran," whispered Roy.

4

Chores and Fun

Fern dressed quickly in the morning. "It's so c-cold," she shivered. She could see her breath as she spoke.

"It's always cold in the mornings up here," said Paw. He handed her a cup of hot brown liquid. "It'll warm up quickly when the sun gets over that range."

At least Fern's hands were warm as she held the steaming coffee.

"Go ahead and drink the coffee, Fern. It'll warm you," said Gran.

Fern took a sip, but it tasted bitter. She made a funny face.

"Here, let me put in a little sugar. I can't drink it black either," said Gran.

Roy joined the group by the fire. Gran handed him a cup of sugared coffee too. "I'm afraid we won't have much milk this summer except for a bit of tinned milk for cooking. We might find a rancher to trade with, though," said Gran.

After a breakfast of bacon and fresh corn bread, Paw announced a family meeting. "We need to decide the jobs you children will have and the rules for the camp," he said. "Do you have any suggestions?"

"I think we should share the jobs around a bit. I really don't like to always have to get the wood," said Roy.

"I don't mind getting wood, but I can't carry the really heavy pieces. And I don't want to always wash the dishes," added Fern.

"Can you two find a way to share the jobs?" Gran asked.

"We sure can," answered Roy and Fern.

"You'll also have to take care of the horses. Paw has to spend most of his time chopping and cutting the logs, and I help him," said Gran.

"Sure," said Roy. Fern nodded her head in agreement.

"Will we have some time to explore?" Roy asked.

"Yes," said Paw. "But I want you to always stay within calling distance of the wagon until you get to know the area. And you must not go up the hill where I'll be cutting."

"Yes, Paw," said the children.

"Before you set to work, Fern, I have something for you," said Gran handing her a package wrapped in brown paper.

Fern looked puzzled as she opened the bundle. She discovered a pair of overalls and a small blue cotton work shirt inside. They were just like Roy's.

She looked up as Gran said, "Can't go running around in a skirt and petticoat up here. Those are better clothes for exploring."

Grinning, Fern dashed off to the wagon to try on her new clothes. Then the children set to work on their chores. They hoped to have some time before lunch to explore the creek.

Fern gathered downed wood in the area. Roy helped her drag in a few big logs that could be cut up for the fire. Roy cleaned up the breakfast dishes.

Gran showed Roy how to dig a sump hole. She explained that it was a place for dirty dishwater. They made sure that the hole was far from the creek. Later Paw would help them dig a hole for an outhouse.

They rearranged the cooking area so that the sitting places were out of the smoke. Then they stored the food in the heavy food locker. Gran said to leave nothing out because the animals would be able to find it.

Fern and Roy carried water from the creek in big buckets. Fern couldn't lift the bucket by herself. But with Roy's help, they lifted it easily.

The horses were fed and groomed. They would do the heavy work of harvesting the poles on the mountain.

By late morning, the children had finished their chores.

"Let's go down to the creek," said Roy. "I saw some willows there. We can make a couple of fishing poles. And Paw has some hooks in this box." He dug around in the box and put some items in his pocket.

"Do we need some worms?" asked Fern. "I saw a soft spot of dirt at the edge of the meadow. There's got to be lots of worms there."

"Good," said Roy. "First, let's go find the best place to fish."

They began to pick their way along the edge of the creek. Rocks scattered across the creek made it easy for them to weave down the hill. They could hear Paw's ax chopping away even over the sound of rushing water. So they knew they hadn't gone too far.

Around a bend, they found the perfect fishing spot. The creek slowed here and formed a deep pool. A large rock bordered one side of the creek. Fallen trees, mossy in the cool shade, made a good seat on the other side.

"I bet there are great fish in this pool," said Fern. She bent over to dip her hand into the still water. "Brrr! It's so cold. I think this water was snow not too long ago."

"Let's go get the willows," said Roy.

They turned and walked back upstream. Roy used his pocketknife to cut two willow branches about four feet long. He stripped off the leaves and small branches. Then he took fishing line, hooks, and lead weights from his pocket.

While Roy made the poles, Fern ran to the nearby meadow. With a stick, she dug a hole to look for worms. She ran back with several worms just a few minutes later. "Hurry up, Roy. They're wiggling in my hand," said Fern.

"Here, wrap them up in this big leaf," Roy said.

Soon the children had returned to the fishing spot. They settled themselves on the logs.

"Does this creek have a name?" asked Fern.

"Don't think so," answered Roy.

"Let's name it then. What are some good names for rivers?" asked Fern.

"Well," said Roy, "in a book I read, there was a river named the Nile and one called the Amazon. They were very far away, though, and a whole lot bigger than this creek."

"Let's call it the Amazon," suggested Fern.

"The Amazon it is, and we'll call this place Crocodile Point," agreed Roy.

Fern looked a little worried and said, "There aren't any crocodiles here, are there?"

"No," laughed Roy. "But there is a big snake sunning himself on that rock across the creek."

Fern started to jump up. She wasn't very fond of snakes.

Roy said, "Don't worry, Fern, it looks like a king snake. It doesn't have a rattle, anyway. I don't think he'll bother us."

The snake, moving very slowly, positioned itself on the warm rock in full sunshine.

"He's trying to warm up enough to move around," Roy explained. "Snakes get very slow when it's cold. He's probably just finished hibernating."

Very slowly, the snake curled himself. He flicked his tongue in and out, trying to sense danger. Fern couldn't help imitating him, sticking her tongue out quickly.

Suddenly there was a tug on Roy's line. "I got one!" shouted Roy.

He grabbed the line and began pulling in a large trout. The underside of the fish glistened with a rainbow of colors.

"Oh, boy. He's so-o big!" said Roy. Roy grabbed at his line and struggled to bring the fish up. It pulled heavily on the line, but finally the fish was wiggling on the mossy bank.

"Oh, he's so pretty," said Fern. Just then her pole gave a mighty tug. "Oh, me too! Me too!" she cried. "Help me, Roy. Help me pull him in."

Fern's pole was almost bent in two as Roy caught the line. He managed to swing Fern's fish next to his on the bank.

"This is fun," said Fern. "Let's catch some more."

"No," said Roy. "We have enough for lunch. That way there will be some for next time."

"Won't Paw, Gran, and Aunt Hattie be proud of us? We caught lunch!" said Fern.

The fish were delicious cooked over the open fire. Roy and Fern shared the biggest one. Gran, Paw, and Aunt Hattie had insisted.

After lunch, Gran gave each of the children a large empty cloth sack and took them into the meadow. She showed them how to gather bunches of dried grass and stuff the sack full.

"This will make a soft, sweet-smelling bed," said Gran. "Make sure you only gather the dried grass. We don't want your bed to be damp."

When the bags were bursting, they dragged them back to camp. Aunt Hattie stitched them shut with a large needle and thread.

"These will last you a few weeks. Then we'll change the grass," Gran said.

That afternoon, the children followed Paw and Gran up the hill. Paw had downed a dozen small pines and had started to clean off the branches. It would be the children's job to carry the branches down the hill. There they would stack them out of the way.

It wasn't too hard to pull the branches down the steep incline, but climbing back up the hill became harder and harder. Fern's lungs burned, and her legs ached.

Paw had gone farther down the hill to chop more saplings. By mid-afternoon, the family was tired and resting in the shade.

"Paw, will you take out the rest of these trees later?" asked Roy. "There's lots more left here that are the right size."

"No," said Paw, "I only take a few from each area. I try to get them all the right size and take ones that are growing close together. Then I look at how straight they are. I leave some of the biggest ones. They will make seeds for new trees."

"Seems like it would be easier work if you just took all of them down," said Fern.

"Well, it would be easier," Paw began. "Then I wouldn't have to worry so much about which way the tree falls. But this is a steep hillside. What do you think would happen if there were no trees on the hill? Look here."

Paw brushed aside the pile of leaves and pine needles that blanketed the ground where they sat. He dug into the soft earth with a stick and made a mound of dirt. Then he took the canteen and poured water over the mound. The water quickly moved the soil mound down the hill.

"If there were no trees, the rain would do this to the whole hill. Where do you think the rain would take the soil, Fern?" asked Paw.

Fern thought for a minute and said, "Into the stream. Into the Amazon?"

Paw smiled. "That's right," he said. He stretched and stood up. "Do you think the fish in the stream would like all that mud?"

"No," said Roy. "They probably couldn't live in muddy water."

"I've been taking pole trees off these hills for almost twenty years," said Paw, looking out over the forest. "I hope that when I'm done it will look very much the same as when I started. It doesn't do for man to make his mark on the land too strongly."

"Or women either," said Fern.

Gran smiled.

The family worked into twilight and then walked tiredly back to camp. Aunt Hattie had a rabbit stew boiling and ready to eat. Everyone was hungry.

Before twilight was replaced by night, the children were asleep on their soft grass beds.

The days that followed were much the same. The children had their chores. The family ate a large breakfast and dinner. And everyone worked to harvest the poles from the forest.

Roy learned to help Paw with the two-man saw. Paw used it to cut the downed poles into sections. Fern had tried it once but ended up getting pulled by the saw instead of pulling it.

Fern was very good, however, at finding just the right tree for Paw to cut next. Sometimes Paw let her shout, "DOWN BELOW!" as one of the trees was felled.

Often there was time to go fishing. And on those days, they had trout for lunch.

5

Exploring

Gran insisted the children wash up each night. They used warm water heated on the fire. "It's been quite a while since you've had a bath," she said. "It's not healthy for children to stay dirty."

One hot afternoon, the family stopped working early. They had decided to take a swim in the creek.

"Ladies first," said Paw, bowing deeply to Fern, Gran, and Hattie.

Paw and Roy stayed in camp while the girls headed to a deep spot in the creek. It felt good to poke a toe in the icy water. But it was slow torture to get wet all over.

After Fern was in, Gran handed her the soap. Fern stood on a mossy rock and scrubbed. Then she made a daring plunge into the deep part.

"Now," said Gran, "let's wash your hair."

"Oh-h," moaned Fern as she dipped her head in the water. "It hurts my head. And I have to do it again to get the soap off."

Fern tingled all over as she dried with the rough towel. "I don't think I've ever been this clean!" she remarked.

Gran and Hattie finished washing, and the three of them walked back to camp. Roy looked worried as Paw started down the hill. "Your turn," smiled Fern, returning the bow.

The days had passed so quickly in the mountains. Fern was surprised when Gran said they had been camping for three weeks. She hadn't missed Ma all that much, except when she awoke in the middle of the night. On those dark nights, she ached for her mother's strong, warm arms. She had to take a deep breath to keep from crying. But a hug from Gran was a big help. And when Aunt Hattie smiled at her, it didn't seem too lonely.

One day Paw lifted Fern up on his strong shoulders and gave her a wild ride around the wide meadow. Gran said she squealed so loudly that everything on the mountain was in hiding.

One morning after breakfast, Paw announced that it was Sunday. "Today, we're going to rest," he said.

After a special breakfast of flapjacks, Paw suggested exploring.

"Let's go explore the Amazon," said Roy. "We haven't been very far up the river."

"I'll pack us a lunch," said Gran. And soon they began their adventure.

Paw made a walking stick for each of them. For the first part, Roy was in the lead.

First, the children shared their special fishing spot, Crocodile Point. Then they wove their way up the riverbank. Sometimes they crossed the river on the large rocks. At one point, they saw deer scampering into the brush. In the wet mud of the riverbank, there were many tracks: raccoon, fox, elk, and even bear.

"Look, Paw," said Roy. "There are lots of chopped tree trunks on the bank over there. Is there someone else getting fence posts up here?"

"No. Those saplings look chewed, not chopped," said Paw. "Look, there's one over here. See how it's gnawed all around the tree and then chewed into small pieces? We've found beavers.

"Sh-h-h," Paw continued. "Remember how I showed you to walk from your toe to heel? Let's see if we can catch them at work."

Quietly, and being careful not to step on twigs, the family worked its way up the river. As they rounded a bend, they saw a large pond before them. The pond had formed because the river was dammed up with large piles of sticks. There were several beavers swimming in the pond. One was carrying a long stick in its mouth.

"We're downwind, so they may not know we're here," Paw whispered. "They use their sense of smell to sense danger. Look over there on that little island in the middle of the river. Do you see the mother with the two kits?"

The children watched as the mother beaver and the two kits munched on small twigs and leaves. The mother was grooming one of the kits. A beaver on the far side of the river was standing on his hind legs, chewing on a small willow tree. He kept pulling chunks out of the trunk, working his way around the base of the tree.

Fern asked quietly, "Paw, what's the large mound of sticks in back of the dam?"

"That's their den," Paw said.

"But how do they get inside? I don't see a way in," whispered Roy.

"The entrance is underwater. That way no other animals can get into it," explained Paw. "They swim up from underneath."

"I think the babies are cute. I wish I could pet one," said Fern.

Gran smiled and said, "I wonder if they're soft."

"They are. That's why there aren't so many beavers around anymore," said Paw. "They've been trapped.

People want their soft fur to make hats."

Roy made a funny face. "Do they put the beaver's tail on the back of the hat?"

Fern started to giggle as she thought of important men wearing beaver tails. Gran started to hush her, but the beavers had been startled. The mother scurried her kits back into the den. The other adults were heading for cover.

Paw stood to go. He smiled and answered, "No. But if they did, maybe fewer people would wear them."

They walked on to a little waterfall and had their picnic there. It got warm enough in the afternoon sunshine for the children to wade in the creek. They pretended to be beavers building a dam in the river. But each time they thought they had the stones and sticks just right, the river would break through and wash them all away.

Wet and muddy, they climbed back onto shore to warm themselves in the sun. Aunt Hattie had found a spot of clover and was tying blossoms together.

"What are you doing, Aunt Hattie?" said Fern. Aunt Hattie motioned for Fern to come closer. She placed a small wreath of clover in Fern's hair.

Roy saw the flowers and made an exaggerated, low bow before Fern. "What is the fair lady's command?" he asked.

Aunt Hattie smiled at the children's antics. She pointed down the hill and made a carrying motion.

Fern understood and giggled, "Aunt Hattie says you could carry me down the hill."

"I left my steed at home today, so I am afraid we will have to walk," sighed Roy.

Aunt Hattie, watching Roy's lips, shrugged and smiled. Then they all began the long walk back down to camp.

Gran was puffing as they reached First Camp. "I'm very glad we went uphill on the way out," she said. "I don't think I would have made it to camp if we'd had to walk uphill on the way back."

The children had learned to watch for the many birds that lived on the mountain. They mostly loved the golden eagle that circled high above them in the twilight. Sometimes they were close enough to hear his high call as it echoed down their canyon.

In the meadow, an unsuspecting rabbit looked up from his dinner of grass to see the poised talons of the eagle. In an instant, a high squeal was all that remained.

Fern sighed for the rabbit. But Aunt Hattie motioned to the eagle's nest high on a cliff across the canyon. She made a motion to say that the baby birds would eat tonight.

"I know, Aunt Hattie. I just feel sorry for the rabbit's family," said Fern.

Hattie nodded in understanding.

6
The Owl

That night, the family went to bed as soon as it was dark. Roy had fallen asleep already and was breathing deeply. Fern lay by the back of the wagon looking out at the stars. They were very bright. The moon had not yet risen. Out over the canyon, she heard a long screech. She thought of the eagle.

All at once, she heard a desperate flapping of small wings and again the screech. This time it was very close. The wagon was filled with wings and cries.

Roy woke with a start and began to yell. Fern screamed and tried to hide herself under the covers. Paw was soon at the back of the wagon trying to see what was happening.

"It's the eagle! The eagle!" shrieked Fern as she and Roy scrambled out the back.

A small bird flew out the front of the wagon. But the plaintive screeching inside the wagon continued.

Paw lit a lantern and peered inside. On a box near the front of the wagon stood a huge owl. Its eyes, round and yellow, blinked in the lantern light. Its wing hung at its side.

"It looks like he must've hurt it when he ran into the wagon cover. Probably hunting that bird," said Paw.

"What will happen to him?" asked Fern.

"We'll have to see if we can heal him up," said Gran. "You children can sleep out here for the rest of the night. There is no way we'll be able to get near him tonight. If he's here in the morning, we'll try to feed him."

Later the children tried to sleep. But the owl continued to cry out through the night.

In the morning, the children watched Aunt Hattie. She placed small pieces of raw meat on a metal plate. Then she carried the plate to the back of the wagon and set it down. The owl screeched in fear as Hattie approached. But hunger soon won out, and the owl hopped down and ate the meat.

"Well, at least he has a chance. He's still eating," said Gran.

―――――――

As morning dawned the next day, the owl was still perched on a crossbar in the front of the wagon. His left wing could stretch and move. But the right one hung limp. When anyone approached, he let out a screech that made Fern cover her ears in pain.

It became Roy's job to bring the raw meat. After a few times, the owl only screeched a bit as Roy slowly approached. Roy always made sure to stay well away from the three-inch talons and hooked beak.

"I think he is getting used to me," said Roy.

Paw looked up from his breakfast and said, "I'm not sure you're doing him any favors. If he can't survive on his own, we shouldn't be helping him."

"But Paw," said Fern, "we're only helping until he's stronger. We can't just let him die."

Paw shook his head and went to get his ax. "On Saturday, we need to go into town. We're out of supplies, and I need to replace that saw blade. The owl has to leave the wagon Saturday morning."

Paw gathered his tools. He and Gran prepared for the day's work.

"That only gives us three days," said Roy as their grandparents hiked away from camp. "His wing will never heal by then."

"We'll have to think of some way to get him out by then. Will he let you next to him?" asked Fern.

"I haven't wanted to get too close," replied Roy.

Hattie looked up from the mending she was doing. First she pointed to the wagon and then put her finger to her lips.

"Yes, Aunt Hattie's right. Why don't you try? He's had his food. Maybe he'll let you in closer if you go slowly," said Fern. Hattie watched and nodded.

Roy pulled together his best brave face and straightened his shoulders. Then he walked slowly toward the wagon. Fern and Hattie sat silently at the fire. Quietly, Roy stood at the back of the wagon and waited for the owl to get used to him. Then he crept up the first makeshift step into the wagon.

The owl bristled his orange and brown feathers and watched with his great, round eyes. After a few moments, Roy mounted the second step and perched on the tail of the wagon.

He sat very still and looked straight at the owl, scarcely breathing. His stomach was a twisted rope inside him. As he sat there, both he and the owl relaxed. He noticed that the owl's feathers began to smooth against his body. Then Roy slowly backed his way out of the wagon and returned to Fern.

"Oh, Roy, I was so scared for you!" whispered Fern. Aunt Hattie nodded.

Each hour, Roy returned to the wagon to visit the owl. By afternoon, he was able to enter the wagon without causing ruffled feathers. And by the time Gran and Paw returned for dinner, Roy was able to get within a few feet of the bird.

Fern had not been idle. After doing her chores and a few of Roy's, she had gone down to the willow grove. She had cut a large pile of long, thin branches. Together, she and Roy had fashioned a triangular shelter and wedged it into a nearby tree. Then they covered it with large leaves.

Paw shook his head as he looked at the shelter and said, "That cage will never hold him, Roy."

"Oh, no, Paw. It's not a cage," explained Roy. "See, there isn't even a door. It's just a shelter for the owl to sit in and stay safe."

"It will keep him cooler too," added Fern, breathlessly.

Paw huffed.

At nightfall, Roy took food to the owl. Then Roy sat within a few feet of the owl and watched him eat. Gran nodded approvingly, and Fern grinned from where she sat back by the fire.

The next day Roy approached the owl, holding a stick close to himself. Each time he returned that day, he edged a bit closer and moved the stick forward. The owl bristled at times but seldom became upset as Roy drew closer and closer.

After dinner, Roy drew himself up and said, "Well, I expect it's time to give this a try."

"Good luck, son," said Paw.

The family sat quietly by the fire as Roy mounted the steps by the wagon. He was holding his now familiar stick. Roy inched forward as he watched the owl looking back at him through the dimming light. The owl ruffled his feathers, slowly moving the healing right wing.

Roy held the stick in front of the huge bird and gently touched its legs with it. As Roy pressed lightly against the legs of the owl, the great bird moved onto the stick and grasped it tightly. Roy moved the stick toward him. Then he walked a few steps toward the back opening. The owl waved his wing in an effort to balance but did not let go. Roy was holding both ends of the stick looking at the owl face-to-face.

"Good boy," whispered Roy. The owl blinked.

Roy made his way down the steps. His arms ached from the weight. Roy scarcely breathed as he inched across the edge of the camp to where the shelter stood.

The owl was looking into Roy's eyes until the bird suddenly caught sight of a bat in the early evening twilight. Roy saw the owl's eyes focus on his prey and follow it through the air. He sensed the owl tensing and saw one wing prepare for flight. But the other wing would not obey. The owl seemed to know he still could not fly. He watched the lucky prey dive away into the night.

With a quick motion, Roy settled the owl into his shelter. The bird was still grasping the stick in his talons. The bottom of the shelter had several other large sticks lashed in, and the owl moved onto one. Roy backed away as the family breathed in relief.

"Nice job, Roy," said Gran.

"We'll see if he can stay there," said Paw.

"Paw, can I stay in camp tomorrow instead of going to town with you? I want to make sure he's all right," said Roy.

"But there's no one to stay with you," said Gran.

Aunt Hattie made a motion to Gran indicating that she would stay with Roy and the owl.

"All right," said Paw, as he checked with Gran. "I guess you three can look out for each other."

The owl gave a piercing screech from his perch. "I think I'll name him *Hoot*," laughed Roy.

"Or *Screech!*" giggled Fern.

7

Trip to Town

Fern woke up before it was light. She was excited to ride into the little town of Barker. She ate a quick breakfast and prepared for the ride.

Gran said to Roy, "It will be after dark before we get back. You take care of camp and try your hand at that stew I showed you. Then we'll have something to eat when we get back."

"Yes, ma'am," said Roy. "Can I go fishing and catch something for the owl?"

"Best not today. Hattie will need your ears. You stay in sight," said Paw.

Roy was a little disappointed. He could see it was going to be a long day. But he just didn't want to leave the owl yet. "Have fun, Fern. Bring me some licorice?"

Fern waved as the wagon rolled away from camp. "I'll get us something," she shouted back.

Roy finished the morning chores. It took longer than he thought. "I guess Fern does help a lot," he said to himself. "I wish I could talk to Hattie. It's lonely here."

Hattie had busied herself with the mending. She was just sewing a button back on Paw's shirt as Roy came back to the sitting area. Hattie had watched his lips moving as he spoke. She nodded her head and pointed to a stump. She wanted him to sit down by her. She began to point to various things around the camp. Then she made a quick sign with her hand. She repeated the action several times before Roy got the idea.

"Hattie, can you teach me the signs?" asked Roy.

Hattie took Roy's face in her hands. Roy repeated the question. Hattie nodded and smiled.

Hattie pointed to the owl and made a quick sign with her hands that looked like a bird. Roy formed the word with his hands. Hattie smiled.

"Show me some more," said Roy.

Throughout the afternoon, they worked and laughed. Roy felt as if he had learned a very special secret code. He could hardly wait to share it with Fern.

———————————

Fern, Paw, and Gran were glad to climb down from the wagon's tall wooden seat. The road had some bruising bumps. They had ridden into town hoping to see a few people, but there were not many about.

They walked into an old wooden shack. It was just a bit larger than the scatter of other buildings in the town. Fern noticed that all the buildings needed painting. A few had even started to fall in. Some were little more than hollow shells clinging to the steep sides of the mountain, their windows gaping.

"Hello, folks. Oh hello, James! Didn't know ya' at first. Who's dis wee 'un?" said the man behind the counter in a funny voice. "Hello, ma'am. Glad ta see ya' again."

"Hello, Mr. MacGinnes. How are you?" replied Gran. "This is our granddaughter, Fern."

"Howdy, MacGinnes," said Paw, clasping the old man's weathered hand. Mr. MacGinnes was a very small man, thin and wiry. A fringe of white hair surrounded his bald head. And a great white beard hung down to his chest.

"Ya' folks'r up for da summer again? Are ya' at Firs' Camp? Haven't been down much since winter. The fish'n

50

still purty good, is it? Don't see many folks up this'r way since da silver played out. Jus' us ol' timers. Store's still all right cuz people still use da road to go into da Rockies. What'cha need?" He took a breath. Fern had never heard anyone talk so fast.

"We will need some flour, sugar, bacon . . ." Gran went on with her list as Fern wandered back through the store.

Although the outside of the store was a disaster, the inside was as neat as Gran's kitchen. All the items were neatly stacked and looked recently dusted. Fern saw wide steel pans on a back shelf. As she picked one up, Paw looked over and said, "Those are for gold panning, Fern."

"Do they catch the gold with a pan?" asked Fern.

"Nope," replied Mr. MacGinnes as he stroked his shiny head. "Da miners used those ta find gold'n da rivers. But there taint' much lef' round these parts. Use'ta be some, ev'n down your way at Firs' Camp. No more, no more."

"How much are they, Mr. MacGinnes?" asked Fern. Maybe they didn't cost much, and she could take one back to Roy.

"How much, missy? How much?" Mr. MacGinnes chuckled. "I use'ta git near five dollars for each one of those. Humpf! Haven't sol' one'n years. What'cha want it fer? No good ta ya' anymore."

Fern sighed and looked dejected.

"Tell ya' what," he said as he knelt down and looked Fern straight in the face. "I'll give it to ya'. We'll make a deal. Ya' find some gold, ya' pay me fer it. Deal, purty miss?" Mr. MacGinnes stuck out his crinkled hand. His eyes were clear blue and smiled back at her. He meant it! Fern stuck out her hand and they shook.

"You don't have to give it to her, MacGinnes," said Paw.

"Naw, naw, I'll never sell 'em. Let her try. Ya' have yer Paw show ya' how ta pan. He knows sumthun 'bout pannin'. He do, he do. Best durn panner these parts ever seen," he said as he looked up at Paw.

"Long ago. Long ago, MacGinnes," said Paw. "That was a different time."

"Yep," replied the old man with a sigh. "Yep."

After the supplies were loaded into the wagon, Mr. MacGinnes said, "Oh, I pert' near forgot your letter. It came a bit ago. Let me see. Where did I put it? Don't get many letters these days fer folks. Ah, here." He handed the letter to Gran who turned and held it out to Fern.

"It's from your ma, Fern. For you and Roy," she said.

Fern took the small letter from Gran and felt the smooth, crisp paper of the envelope.

"I never got my own letter before," Fern said. She wanted to tear into it then and there, but it was for Roy too. It said so on the envelope. "I'll just hold it until we get back to First Camp, and we can read it together."

Paw climbed back onto the high wooden seat of the wagon. Fern scrambled in between him and Gran and held onto her letter. Mr. MacGinnes handed her the pan.

"Good luck, now, purty miss," he said, grinning. "Have a safe trip an' come'n see me again, folks." Fern waved to the old man.

Paw clicked to the horses and slapped the reins on their backs. They were off with a lurch, rumbling down the path and out of the sad old town.

Fern thought they would never get home. Every time she looked down at the letter she carefully held, her heart gave a little skip. She had forgotten how much she missed her mother. She longed to be cuddled by her and sung to sleep. She could hear her mother's sweet voice, "Sing low, sweet chariot, comin' forth to carry me home . . ."

"Fern, we're back. You fell asleep," whispered Gran in her ear.

It was dark. Fern could just make out the campfire ahead as the wagon groaned to a stop in the clearing. Roy was calling to her as he ran forward.

8
Ma's Letter

"Ma sent a letter," shouted Fern, suddenly fully awake. "I saved it so we could read it together. Can we read it now, Paw? And I brought you a present, Roy."

"Let's read the letter by the fire," said Gran as she climbed down from the wagon. "The supplies can wait until morning."

The family gathered by the fire. Gran hugged Hattie and sat down.

"Hattie and I baked some biscuits for you, and I found some strawberries by the river. We saved them for you," said Roy. "Hattie and I had a good time. She showed me some words in her sign language. We can talk now."

Gran smiled at Roy and thanked him as she took a biscuit.

Paw had unhitched the horses and given them their feed. He rubbed them down quickly and left them to munch sweet grass in their temporary corral. He returned to the fire as the rest of the family enjoyed the sweet biscuits.

"Here are some for you, Paw," said Roy.

"Now, Fern, where's that letter?" Paw said as he took a biscuit.

Paw read aloud.

July 28

The Brown Palace Hotel
Denver, Colorado

My darling children,

   I can't tell you how hard it was to say good-bye to you. The only thing that helped was that I knew this summer would be something you'd treasure your whole life. It will be something to tell your grandchildren about. I remember First Camp and the beautiful river nearby from the times that I went with your grandparents. Have you caught any fish yet? Did you find the cave?

My work here is fine. The head cook in the kitchen is from France. He makes some of the most interesting foods. The people in the restaurant love his cooking. He's very hard to understand, and sometimes we have disagreements. But one day he was very busy, and he let me bake apple pies for dessert! They named it a funny French name, but it was still apple pie. He thought they were wonderful, and now I'm his assistant. I'm learning a great deal, but my feet are very tired at the end of the evening.

I want you to know that when you return later this summer to Denver, we won't be going back to live with Gran and Paw again. Do you remember Mr. Arnold? I introduced you before you left. We've spent some time together this summer and decided we'd like to be a family. I want you to have time to get to know John, and I hope you'll love him.

He's a farmer, and he has a small homestead not too far from Gran and Paw's. It's near the town of Buffalo, about half-a-day's ride. He's gone back now to work the land and to finish the house for us. He'll come back to meet you in the fall. I know this a big surprise, but I wanted you to have time to think about it before you come back to Denver.

*I think of you every minute of every day and
miss you with all my heart. Now go find that cave
and have a wonderful Rocky Mountain Summer.*

Love, Ma

Paw folded the letter and placed it in the envelope,
sighing. Gran was smiling and made some signs to Aunt
Hattie, even though Hattie had watched Paw's lips. Soon
Aunt Hattie was smiling too.

Roy was having a hard time understanding why
everyone was smiling. He didn't want to go anywhere
else, and he sure didn't want to have a new dad. Ma was
enough.

Fern looked over at him and said, "I liked that man,
Mr. Arnold. He has kind eyes. I think it'll be all right,
Roy."

Roy brushed a tear that rolled slowly down his cheek.
His throat was too tight to say anything. He just walked
away from the fire and sat on a log.

"Give him a little time, Fern," said Gran.

Hattie rose and silently moved over next to Roy. She
sat quietly next to him as Roy leaned over and cried onto
her shoulder.

Fern felt that squeezy feeling in her heart. She felt it
when she thought too much about missing her mom. She
tried to push it away and took a deep breath. But as she
looked at her brother's shaking shoulders, she felt what
he was feeling.

Gran gave her a nudge and said, "I think I know where that cave is that your ma was talking about. Maybe Paw could go with you tomorrow and scout it for you. He can make sure it's still safe. I remember your ma and your Aunt Mary used to spend a lot of time up there."

Roy looked over at Gran and Paw and asked, through his tears, "Do you think we could?"

9
The Cave

It started to rain early the next morning. Fern awoke to a great clap of thunder that rolled down the river valley. Raindrops splattered on the wagon's canvas cover. A cool, damp breeze ruffled through the wagon.

When a big drop plopped on Fern's nose, she decided she should get up. Paw had fixed up a shelter near the fire. Paw, Gran, and Aunt Hattie were huddled under it now.

The fire hissed and smoked but was still warm and inviting. Fern made a dash for the shelter. Aunt Hattie filled a blue tin cup with a wonderful-smelling brown liquid. Fern sipped it and smacked her lips.

"Oh, what is this, Gran? It tastes so wonderful!" said Fern.

"Aunt Hattie warmed some of the tinned milk we bought in Barker. Then she mixed it with sugar and a chunk of chocolate. It's good, isn't it?" replied Gran.

Fern turned to Aunt Hattie and said, "Thank you, Aunt Hattie. It's delicious!"

Hattie signed to Fern, "You are welcome."

To Fern, Hattie's signing seemed more like talking now. It was just like hearing her say the words.

"Looks like it's going to rain most of the morning," sighed Paw.

"Well, never mind," said Gran. "We've had more than our fair share of good weather. It's been weeks since it really rained up here. Even the river was a bit down. Let's have a big breakfast. I'll make hotcakes and bacon. Then we'll see what the day brings."

Fern was so full of Gran's huge pancakes she could hardly run back to the wagon. She settled in her soft bed of grasses and curled up in two quilts. Roy was not far behind her. As he entered the wagon, he shook his head very hard. Drops of water splattered everywhere.

"Watch out, Roy! You're as bad as the rainstorm!" squealed Fern.

Roy grinned and settled into his nest. "Hoot is doing fine. The shelter is keeping him dry. I put up a couple of branches to block the wind. He sure eats a lot now!"

"I'm glad he's getting better," said Fern.

She hesitated and then said in a whisper, "What do you think about Ma's letter?"

Roy's smile vanished. He whispered back, "I'm scared, I guess. I really don't know Mr. Arnold very well. I was with Paw most of the times that Mr. Arnold came by. He seems fine. But as a dad that's different."

Fern thought a moment and said, "I know it will be different, but I watch Ma sometimes. She looks so sad when she thinks I'm not looking. And she smiles differently when Mr. Arnold is around. Maybe we should just wait and see. You know what Ma says about choosing how you look at things. Let's just wait and see and not worry."

Roy sighed as he settled back and said, "Do you remember our father, Fern?"

"No, not really," replied Fern.

"I think I do," said Roy. "I just remember a big man who picked me up. But I can't remember his face. You were only one when we left. But I was three."

"I wish I could remember. But maybe Mr. Arnold will be a good memory too."

It rained five days straight, and it never stopped once. Fern had never seen it rain so much. Once in a while, there would be a clap of thunder. But most of the time, it just rained.

Roy was learning how to whittle a small animal out of a stick. Aunt Hattie had brought out some needlework. Fern was so tired of the rain that she asked Aunt Hattie to show her how to do the stitches. She even had a little needlework of her own to do. It was a handkerchief with flowers. If it didn't stop raining soon, though, she was afraid that she would stick all of her fingers with the needle.

"I think I might be better at whittling," said Fern. "This is hopeless."

Gran smiled at Fern as she struggled to get the needle to go where she wanted.

"Never mind," laughed Gran. "I struggle with needlework too. Hattie is the one with the gift. If you would rather whittle, it's fine with me. I'll show you how."

The next morning, the light streaming inside the wagon woke Fern up. At first she couldn't decide what was different about this morning. Then she realized that nothing was dripping. She gave Roy a quick nudge and struggled into her overalls. She was out the back of the wagon before Roy had managed to sit up.

"Come on, slug-a-bed. The sun is shining!" cheered Fern.

Roy gave a whoop of joy and soon joined her in the fresh morning air. The sky was so blue that it almost hurt their eyes to look at it.

"Let's go find that cave today, Fern," suggested Roy. "I know we'll have a lot of chores to catch up on. But after that, I bet Gran would let us."

"Great!" said Fern. "Where do we start?"

Before he left with his ax, Paw said, "I believe that cave is up above the spot where you kids fish, just across the river. It's pretty steep up there. If you find the opening, come and get me. I'll check it out for you. You don't want to run into a bear or a wildcat."

It seemed that chores took extra long that day. But Hattie offered to feed the horses and pack them a lunch.

Fern and Roy hiked down to the fishing spot and ate their lunch on a warm rock. Roy had his pole in while they ate. He caught three small fish.

"At least Hoot will have something fresh to eat. He doesn't much like biscuits," Roy said.

"Hello, Rex," Fern called to the huge king snake that they had seen many times. He was sunning on the other side of the river again. Fern knew now that he was harmless. She liked the way he slithered slowly away when she disturbed him.

It took a while for the children to discover the best way across the river. They finally had to go upstream a little way to cross. Then they doubled back across from the fishing spot.

Roy led the way as they started to climb the steep hill. It seemed to Fern that in some spots they were going straight up.

"I sure don't see any caves," Fern said, trying to catch her breath.

"It's probably overgrown with vines. Try carefully moving the plants around, but watch out for the brambles," said Roy.

Finally, Roy gave a shout, "I think I found it!"

Fern struggled over to where Roy was standing. She helped him pull the vines and brush away from the entrance.

The cave had a nearly round opening. The children could see a large room inside.

"It doesn't look like anything uses this for a home," said Roy. "I'll go in and check it out."

Before she had a chance to object, Roy had pushed himself into the cave. Fern grabbed his ankles and shouted, "Don't you dare, Roy. Gran and Paw will never let us play in there if you disobey!"

Roy reappeared, "Oh, all right. I suppose we should go get Paw."

The children scrambled down the hill. They picked their way across the river and soon were back at camp.

"We found it! We found it!" they shouted together.

"Good for you," said Gran. "Maybe Paw can go and see it in the morning."

The children's faces fell. "Oh, Gran, can we go now? Please," moaned Fern.

Gran laughed and said, "No. Your paw works too hard to go looking at caves at the end of the day. Why don't you go up and help him a bit now before dinner. That way he'll have some time in the morning to help you."

The children ran off to find Paw before Gran had even finished. They worked with Paw until the light had long disappeared behind the mountain. The first star was just peeping out.

Paw agreed to check out the cave first thing in the morning since the children had been such a big help. Fern didn't think she would be able to sleep a wink. But before she knew it, it was morning.

Paw, Fern, and Roy set off for the cave after a quick breakfast. Gran said she would finish some chores around camp with Hattie.

The children showed Paw the route to the cave. After they crossed the river, Paw suggested, "I think we can tie a rope over that big branch up there. Then you could swing across the fishing spot and make this an easier trip."

"Do you think we could do that?" asked Fern, looking a bit worried.

"If I remember right, that was how your ma did it. She thought up the idea. Now let's see the cave," said Paw.

They scrambled up the steep hill. Soon they stood at the entrance of the cave trying to catch their breath in the thin mountain air.

Paw looked around the opening and said, "You're right, Roy. It doesn't look like anything uses the cave. It doesn't smell of bear." He lit a candle and continued, "You stay right here. I'll look inside."

His feet disappeared. A few moments later, he called to the children to follow him. Roy dove through the opening and called back to Fern, "Come on, Fern. It's not even very dark in here."

Fern scuttled through the opening into a small room.

A ray of light from a hole above lit the room. The floor was littered with rocks. But one small area had been cleared. A small wooden shelf leaned sideways against the wall. It was built of large rocks and an old warped board. Cans were stacked on top with old papers underneath.

Roy shouted, "Hello!" and echoes bounced back at them.

"Ouch, Roy," cried Fern. "I think we'll have to speak softly in here."

"Sorry," said Roy.

"I don't think there's been anything in here since your ma," said Paw. "It started raining that last summer she was here. We had to get back home. She never made it back up here to get her playthings."

"All the cans are empty, Paw," exclaimed Roy. He picked up a faded can of beans.

"Sure," said Paw. "Your gran would give the cans to the girls after we had eaten what was in them. Don't know what she used them for."

"She played store with them," said Fern. "That's what she did."

It felt strange to Roy and Fern to be in the cave. Especially since their ma had played there when she was a little girl.

"Can we stay and fix it up, Paw?" pleaded Roy. "We don't have any chores. Unless you want us to help you."

"Is it safe?" asked Fern.

"Oh, sure," Paw assured her. "Now that our scent is in the place, the animals won't come near. And the walls and ceiling are solid. You two have fun, but be back to help Gran with dinner."

"Yes, Paw," the children answered together.

Paw crawled out the door and walked back down the hill.

The children spent the afternoon arranging and rearranging the rocks. They built a pretend fire. And they decorated the cave with flowers and branches from the hill.

The cave remained cool even as the afternoon sun warmed the hillside. Twice, the children walked down to the river to drink from the stream.

"I guess we'd better head back," said Roy. He noticed that the sun was starting to dip behind the tall peak to the west. "Maybe we can come back tomorrow. I need to catch some more fish for Hoot in the morning."

They heard a rifle shot and then another. "Maybe there'll be rabbit for dinner," Fern said.

The children scrambled down the hill and back to camp.

10

Hoot Goes Free

Roy took Hoot a fish that he had caught earlier in the morning. Hoot was restless. He kept stretching his wings. Both wings seemed to move well now.

"I think," said Gran, "that Hoot needs a bit more room. Why don't you try to get him on the carrying stick. You can carry him out into the meadow."

"Do you think he can fly now?" asked Fern.

"I wouldn't be surprised," said Gran.

Roy got the stick and walked slowly toward Hoot. Hoot remembered how to grasp it with his talons. He climbed on the stick and sat very still. Roy walked the great owl slowly into the green meadow. He gently settled the bird on a fallen tree that stuck out of the tall, waving grass. The bird flapped his wings a few times to gain his balance. Then Hoot settled down, blinking his huge yellow eyes against the bright light.

Hoot seemed unsure of what to do next. Roy knew that Hoot needed to exercise his injured wing. So he began waving his arms toward the owl.

Hoot rose up as he stretched his legs. He spread out his wings. Catching the breeze, he made a gentle glide a few feet forward onto the soft grass.

"Go on, Hoot," whispered Roy.

Hoot rose again into the breeze and flapped his wings. Again he rose into the air. This time he soared higher and higher. He gave a great screech, and the children began to cheer. Hoot circled and landed in a tall pine overlooking the meadow.

Suddenly Roy stopped cheering and said quietly, "See you around, Hoot."

Gran could hear the catch in Roy's voice and gave him a great big hug. Fern was still cheering and calling to Hoot up in the tree.

"Let's give him some time to remember how to be an owl," said Gran. "He knows where we are if he needs us."

As he did his chores, Roy kept glancing up to the top of the pine tree. He wanted to make sure that Hoot was still around.

Roy had promised to help Paw with dragging limbs. He trudged up the hill with a lonesome heart.

"We let Hoot go," Roy said to Paw with a sigh and a brave smile.

"That was best," said Paw quietly. "You did a wonderful job of healing him, Roy. I really never thought that he would make it. You should be proud."

"Thanks, Paw. I'm glad he's well. But I liked having him too," sighed Roy.

"You never *have* a wild creature, Roy. But sometimes you're lucky and get to know one," said Paw.

After a moment, Paw said, "Roy, we have all these limbs and there's a lot of dry wood. What would you think of having a big bonfire tonight? The rains made sure that it would be safe to burn. Would you like to celebrate Hoot's freedom?"

Roy's face brightened like a fresh new morning. "Oh yes, Paw! Where can we have it? What do I do? Is it like a party? Can Fern help?"

"Sure, son," laughed Paw. "I guess you like the idea. Let's get everyone to drag this pile down to the meadow. Then we'll gather some dry wood to give it a good start."

"I'll go tell everyone!" shouted Roy over his shoulder. He started back down the hill. Then suddenly, he stopped and ran back to Paw. He gave Paw a huge hug around the middle and then dashed off with a whoop.

The family joined in the spirit of the bonfire. Fern gathered dry wood and pine cones to begin the blaze. She stacked them in a cone-shaped pile. Roy walked up and down the hill with the long limbs. Paw chopped the biggest limbs into smaller pieces. Gran decided to prepare a feast for the party. And Aunt Hattie mysteriously disappeared for an hour.

As the long twilight approached, the family gathered for supper. Hoot was still perched in the high pine. They heard him call as the moon rose in a perfect crescent.

Aunt Hattie surprised the children with the first of the wild blackberries.

Paw rose to light the bonfire. Slowly, the flames rose as the pine cones burned with color. The green limbs began to hiss and snap. The flames grew taller than the children.

Fern stood back as the heat warmed her face. Roy played at the edge of the light created by the fire. He dodged the smoke that seemed to chase him. His shadow danced on the backdrop of tall pines. The adults settled at a polite distance.

Roy heard a screech overhead from the party's guest of honor. Hoot, spotting a bat, had taken flight and caught it.

Roy let out a screech as loud as Hoot's. He pointed to the bird as it returned to the tall pine with its prey.

"Good job, Hoot!" he called to his friend.

11

The Treasure

The children were picking berries one morning by the Amazon. Roy was best at finding the really sweet berries but usually popped most of them into his mouth.

"Roy, if you don't stop snitching, we'll never get a bucketful for dinner," laughed Fern. But she had a little berry juice on her chin too.

"There are so many berries, I don't think we could eat them all if we tried," said Roy as he wolfed another handful of the shiny purple berries.

"I haven't had a chance to try the pan you got for me in Barker, Fern," said Roy.

"Let's ask Paw how to pan for gold at lunchtime," suggested Fern. "Mr. MacGinnes said Paw used to pan for gold."

Roy pulled the heavy, flat pan from the wagon as Gran called them for lunch.

"Paw, can you show us how to do this?" asked Roy. "We want to see if there's any gold in the Amazon."

Paw huffed and frowned. He said, "Panning is hard, cold work. I'm not sure you'll like it."

Roy and Fern looked downcast. Paw continued with a sigh, "Stand in a part of the river where the water slows a bit. Scoop a handful of sand from the bottom of the river and put it in the pan with lots of water. Swish the pan around. Slosh the lighter pieces of sand and dirt out of the pan."

Paw demonstrated swirling the pan in his hands. "The idea is that the gold is heavier. It'll settle to the bottom if it's sloshed around. The gold, if there is any," said Paw doubtfully, "will be tiny, shiny flecks in the black sand. You'd better borrow my rubber boots. Go ahead, give it a try if you like. But watch out for gold fever."

"I wonder what gold fever is?" said Fern. The children were headed to the river after lunch. "Maybe you catch it because your feet get cold in the water."

"I think it means you get very excited about gold. And then you can't think about anything else," said Roy.

After several hours, the children's feet and hands were freezing. Their backs ached from bending over and holding the heavy pan. Worse yet, the children had not found even a fleck of gold.

"No wonder gold is so valuable," sighed Roy. He heaved himself from the river and pulled off the huge boots. He sat by Fern on the mossy bank.

Fern looked up and noticed that the sky had gone charcoal gray with heavy storm clouds. A distant rumble warned the children.

Roy looked up and said, "I don't think we can get back to camp. The lightning will be here soon! Let's get to the cave!"

They each swung across the river on the rope Paw had tied. Then they raced up the side of the hill and over to the entrance of the cave. They crawled into the cave just as huge drops of rain began to pelt them. A streak of lightning lit the dark sky.

"That one came up fast," said Fern. She shook the rain from her long braids.

Roy peeked out of the cave and watched the hail falling and covering the ground. It looked like hundreds of bouncing white balls.

"It won't last long. But it's a good thing we got here quickly!" said Roy. He settled back near the cave opening to wait out the storm.

Fern wandered around the edge of the cave. She covered her ears each time the thunder boomed. It seemed very loud in the cave.

It was darker in the cave today, but Fern could still make her way around. She kicked something with her foot. Thinking it was just another rock, she tried to push it aside with her toes. It made a funny rattling sound. She reached down and picked up a small metal box that was nearly buried in the dirt.

"Look, Roy. Maybe it's a treasure box," she said. She carried it to the door to get a better look.

Roy shook the box. It rattled.

"It has a little lock," he said.

"Do you think we should open it?" asked Fern. "Maybe we should take it to Gran."

"The rain has almost stopped," said Roy, looking out the entrance. "Let's head back. We can have Paw open it. If it was Ma's, we don't want to break it."

Fern carried the box carefully. Roy picked up clean hail and shared some with Fern. The hailstones melted quickly in their mouths. The hundreds of white balls on the ground quickly disappeared as the sun returned.

Gran, Paw, and Aunt Hattie were very glad to see the children return safe and dry. Fern and Roy showed them the little box. Paw soon had it open with his penknife.

"I remember that box, Paw," said Gran with a smile. "Marie was so upset that she couldn't go back and get her treasures in the cave." Gran continued to Fern and Roy,

"Your ma loved to collect little things. She kept them all in that treasure box. We had to leave it behind one year— the year it rained so hard. I guess she never went back to get it."

"Oh look, Roy," said Fern. "Pretty rocks."

"Fool's gold," said Paw. "Lots of it up here. See how it flakes in flat sheets?"

Many of the pieces were as thin as paper. They were shiny black and gold. "Well, it's not a valuable treasure. But I think I'll take it to Ma as a present anyway. Would you like to see it, Aunt Hattie?" said Fern, offering the box to the quiet woman.

Aunt Hattie took the box and examined each piece. She took one out and looked at it more closely. She motioned to Paw. He took it and looked at it very carefully.

"Well, well, well!" said Paw with a grin. "Looks like your gold hunt has been successful." He bit the small rock with his teeth. "Look, Gran! It's a little nugget!"

Roy gave a whoop of delight, and Fern began to shout, "Really, Paw, really? It's gold?"

"It sure is. I wonder where she found it?" laughed Paw. He handed the nugget to Gran.

"Gran, you save it for Ma. It'll be a wonderful surprise," said Fern.

Roy agreed, "I can't wait to see her."

"Well, it's only a few more days," said Gran. "Right, Paw? We need to be back before a chance of first snow.

The nights have been getting longer and colder."

Paw agreed. "I'll go to Barker tomorrow and get MacGinnes. He'll help us haul the poles back to Denver. He'll need to put up supplies for winter. He can bring a few hands, and we can be on our way in a few days."

"Oh," said Fern, suddenly sad. "I really like it here. I want to see Ma, but I don't want the summer to be over."

"Make the most of the next few days then," said Paw.

Paw rode to Barker the next day, taking one of the horses. He returned at sunset with Mr. MacGinnes and a hired hand.

The next day, the three men loaded and tied the huge pile of poles that had grown through the summer. By the time they had finished, both wagons were stacked to the very top of the canvas. Any supplies that were left were lashed to the sides in boxes or hung off the back.

"Where will we sit?" asked Fern. She was looking up at the loaded wagon. Even the front seat had blankets piled on it.

"We can take turns riding, Fern. It's all downhill. It'll be a very quick trip," said Paw. "MacGinnes, did you check those brakes? These wagons are pretty heavy this time."

"Yep," shouted Mr. MacGinnes. "They'll hold. Let's leave at firs' light."

12

Hello, Ma!

Fern and Roy slept by the fire just as they had the first night in the mountains. They would leave for Denver at dawn.

As the children closed their eyes, they heard Hoot in the distance. He was calling to another owl.

The morning was crisp and clear. Only a small fire burned to warm coffee and hands. When they were ready to leave, the fire was doused and the rocks were scattered.

Roy looked around and said, "It doesn't look like anyone was ever here."

"Exactly," said Paw.

They pulled out of First Camp before the sun came over the towering mountain. Fern and Roy looked back to the big meadow and the tall pine.

"See you next year," called Roy.

The road down the mountain was dusty. As the sun rose above the mountain, the day soon warmed.

They stopped and rested a while at the bent tree. Then the children went ahead to check the road. As they walked along in silence, Fern noticed the aspens on the hill. Once green, they had begun to change to a shimmery gold that twinkled in the sunlight.

Fern walked back up the hill. This time walking up the hill didn't seem as hard as it had in the spring. She was barely puffing as she returned with the all-clear signal.

This was the steepest part of the road. Gran guided the horses, and Paw sat next to her. He held the brake with all his might. Mr. MacGinnes followed at a safe distance. Fern walked with Aunt Hattie behind the wagons.

"I want you out of the way," said Paw.

By the time they reached the bottom, Paw was drenched with sweat. But he smiled and said, "The rest is easy."

Above them, the marmots screeched good-bye.

The travelers reached the river just as the moon rose.

"We'll cross in the morning," said Paw. He slowly climbed down from the wagon, stiff and tired.

———————

After eating a warm breakfast the next morning, they were ready to cross the river. It seemed so narrow and low after seeing it at spring melt.

Paw and Mr. MacGinnes rode up and down the side of the river. They were looking for the best place to cross. They settled on a narrow and slightly deeper spot that wasn't so muddy.

"We don't want 'da wagons stuck in no muddy spot," said Mr. MacGinnes. Paw agreed.

The children piled aboard the wagon. The horses splashed out into the water.

"Don't we need the mules to pull us?" asked Roy.

"No," said Paw as he urged the horses forward with a click of his tongue. "The water is not nearly as deep or fast. We can make it across just fine on our own. Sometimes the river is even dry by this time of year. Sometimes it's just mud. This is a good crossing."

The horses strained under the load. But with Paw shouting at them, they soon climbed the far riverbank. Fern and Roy had dry shoes on this crossing.

It seemed strange to wave and call to people passing on the busy road into Denver. They had seen so few people all summer. Fern wondered what it would be like when they arrived back in the busy city.

The city drew closer on the horizon. As they descended the last few foothills, Fern said, "I'm so excited, Roy. I can't wait to see Ma."

Gran smiled and said to the children, "What do you think was the most wonderful part of the summer?"

Fern answered immediately. "Finding the box in the cave!"

Roy considered Gran's question for a moment. Then he replied, "It has to be Hoot flying into the wagon. I'll never forget him."

"Don't ever forget this summer," said Gran, wistfully.

Hattie signed to Gran, and Gran returned her smile.

"Yes," Gran said. "It's been a wonderful summer."

Paw nodded in agreement.

As the family rode the last mile into town, they passed tall buildings and many coaches, wagons, and carriages.

Fern wondered about the changes in their future. What would it be like with a new dad? Would they get to see Gran, Paw, and Aunt Hattie as Ma had promised? What would their new home be like?

Then Fern saw her ma standing on the boardwalk outside the hotel. Ma was waving and smiling.

They finally pulled up beside Ma. "Fern! Roy! I've missed you so!" she said.

Fern squealed with delight and jumped off the wagon straight into her ma's arms. A flurry of hugs and kisses followed. Everyone was talking at once. They were all laughing and crying.

Ma noticed that Roy hung back a bit from the group.

"Roy," she said, smiling. "How strong you look. You've grown into a man this summer."

Roy knew he wasn't quite all grown yet as he rushed into her strong arms.

"I'm glad to see you, Ma. I missed you," he said softly.

"We have a present for you, Ma. Something you left in the funny little box in the cave. Do you remember?" chattered Fern. She handed over the small metal box.

"I remember," said Ma. "But it was just some old fool's gold."

"Not quite all," chimed in Roy.

Ma opened the box to find the small golden nugget wrapped in a partially embroidered handkerchief.

"We want you to make it into a wedding ring," said Fern.

Roy nodded. Ma looked over to a tall man who had been watching the family reunion. He moved to Ma's side and smiled at the children.

"Hello, Mr. Arnold," said Roy as he stuck out his hand.

Ma looked at her children and smiled, "You *have* grown up this summer."